2020 Monarch Nominee

THE TRUTH ABOUT
BEARS

THE TRUTH ABOUT
BEARS

Maxwell Eaton III

A NEAL PORTER
ROARING BROO[K]
NEW YORK

Copyright © 2018 by Maxwell Eaton III
A Neal Porter Book
Published by Roaring Brook Press
Roaring Brook Press is a division of Holtzbrinck
Publishing Holdings Limited Partnership
175 Fifth Avenue, New York, NY 10010
The art for this book was created using pen and ink with digital coloring.
mackids.com

ISBN: 978-1-62672-666-6
Library of Congress Control Number: 2017944676

FOR EEE

Our books may be purchased in bulk for promotional, educational, or business use. Please
contact your local bookseller or the Macmillan Corporate and Premium Sales Department at
(800) 221-7945 ext. 5442 or by e-mail at MacmillanSpecialMarkets@macmillan.com.

First edition, 2018
Book design by Kristie Radwilowicz

Printed in China by Shaoguan Fortune Creative Industries Co. Ltd.,
Shaoguan, Guangdong Province

1 3 5 7 9 10 8 6 4 2

The three most common bears are:

Polar bears live only in the Arctic.

Bears can be found everywhere except Antarctica, Africa, and Australia.

Bears like to eat . . .

mostly nuts and berries.

They also eat fish,

large animals,

and rodents.

Polar bears eat seals. They smell them
through the seals' breathing holes
in the ice and snow.

Sometimes they smash the ice and grab them.

When a bear is born, it weighs less than a guinea pig.

An adult bear can weigh as much as a small car!

But that doesn't mean we should drive one.

Some bears sleep all winter.

They don't even go to
the bathroom!

Bears have lots of fur.

They use it
as camouflage.

The good news is that you can help
by learning about bears and
then teaching others.

Because bears are incredible animals.

BEAR SAFETY

BEARS AND PEOPLE DON'T MIX. IF YOU EVER SEE A BEAR OUTSIDE, DO NOT RUN.

Hey, who is that?

BEARS ARE FAST.

AND DO NOT CLIMB A TREE.

Where are you going?

BEARS ARE GREAT CLIMBERS.

BEAR FILE

TRACKS

Bear Habitats

Forest
Desert
Water
Sea ice
Alpine tundra
Tropical forest
Grassland
Bamboo forest

FUR

Brown Bear   4 feet

FIELD NOTES

- Eating berries
- Scratching back on tree
- Talking to human child?!

Get more sleep!!!

Further Research

BOOKS FOR CUBS

Bears, Deborah Hodge, illustrated by Pat Stephens, Kids Can Press, 1996.

Bears in the Forest, Karen Wallace, illustrated by Barbara Firth, Candlewick Press, 1994.

Wild about Bears, Jeannie Brett, Charlesbridge, 2014.

BOOKS FOR FULL-SIZED BEARS

National Audubon Society Field Guide to North American Mammals, John O. Whitaker, Jr., 2nd ed., Knopf, 1996.

NOLS Bear Essentials: Hiking and Camping in Bear Country, John Gookin and Tom Reed, Stackpole Books, 2009.

Polar Bears: A Complete Guide to Their Biology and Behavior, Andrew E. Derocher, Johns Hopkins University Press, 2012.

The Bear Almanac, Gary Brown, The Lyons Press, 2009.